A VISIT TO Italy

REVISED AND UPDATED

NORTH AMERICA

SOUTH AMERICA

AUSTRALIA

Rachael Bell

Heinemann
LIBRARY

www.heinemann.co.uk/library
Visit our website to find out more information about Heinemann Library books.

To order:
 Phone 44 (0) 1865 888066
📄 Send a fax to 44 (0) 1865 314091
💻 Visit the Heinemann Bookshop at www.heinemann.co.uk/library to browse our catalogue and order online.

First published in Great Britain by Heinemann Library, Halley Court, Jordan Hill, Oxford OX2 8EJ, part of Pearson Education. Heinemann is a registered trademark of Pearson Education Ltd.

© Pearson Education Ltd 1998, 2008

Editorial: Diyan Leake
Design: Joanna Hinton-Malivoire and Philippa Jenkins
Picture research: Mica Brancic
Production: Duncan Gilbert

Originated by Chroma Graphics (Overseas) Pte Ltd
Printed and bound in China by South China Printing Co. Ltd

ISBN 978 0 431 087320 (hardback)
12 11 10 09 08
10 9 8 7 6 5 4 3 2 1

ISBN 978 0 431 087467 (paperback)
12 11 10 09 08
10 9 8 7 6 5 4 3 2 1

British Library Cataloguing in Publication Data
Bell, Rachael, 1972 –
   A visit to Italy. – New ed.
   1. Italy – Social conditions – 21st century – Juvenile literature 2. Italy – Geography – Juvenile literature 3. Italy – Social life and customs – 21st century – Juvenile literare
I. Title II. Italy
945'.093

Acknowledgements
The publishers would like to thank the following for permission to reproduce photographs: © Axel Poignant Archive p. **29** (Ali Reale); © Colorific p. **22** (David Levenson/Black Star); © Colorsport p. **24**; © Corbis pp. **13** (Reuters/Tony Gentile), **22** (Silvia Morara); © Hutchison Library pp. **23** (J. Davey), **25** (Isabella Tree); © J. Allan Cash pp. **9**, **17**, **21**; © Katz Pictures p. **14** (A. Tosatto); © Performing Arts Library p. **28** (Gianfranco Fainello); © Photolibrary p. **5** (PhotoDisc/John A. Rizzo); © Punchstock p. **12** (Digital Vision); © Robert Francis p. **18**; © Robert Harding Picture Library/Mike Newton pp. **12**, **20**; © Stock Market p. **10**; © Telegraph Colour Library pp. **6** (J. Sims), **8**, **16** (J. Sims); © Tony Stone p. **11** (Joe Cornish); © Trevor Clifford p. **16**; © Trip pp. **7** (R. Cracknell), **15** (P. Nicholas), **20** (W. Jacobs), **26** (W. Jacobs), **27** (H. Rogers).

Cover photograph reproduced with permission of © Lonely Planet Images (Glenn Beanland).

Our thanks to Nick Lapthorn for his comments in the preparation of this book.

Every effort has been made to contact copyright holders of any material reproduced in this book. Any omissions will be rectified in subsequent printings if notice is given to the publishers.

Contents

Any words appearing in bold, **like this**, are explained in the Glossary.

Italy

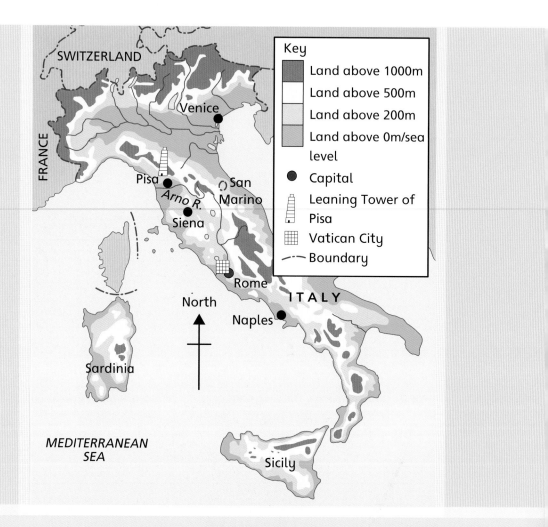

Italy is in southern **Europe**. On a map it looks like a boot sticking out into the Mediterranean Sea. Sicily and Sardinia are islands that are part of Italy.

About 150 years ago, different areas joined up to make Italy. There are still two places inside Italy that are not part of it. They are the Vatican City and San Marino.

The Arno River flows through the city of Florence.

Land

Most of the land in Italy is mountains or hills. These have only thin soil. Farming is difficult here. Many plants cannot grow in thin soil.

In the south of Italy it can get very hot and there is very little rain. The highest mountains are in the north.

Some mountains have snow on them all year round.

Landmarks

One of Italy's most famous buildings is the Leaning Tower of Pisa. It is over 800 years old. There are 294 steps to the top of the tower.

This statue was carved over 500 years ago by a sculptor called Michelangelo.

The Vatican City is like a small, separate town inside Rome. It is the home of the **Pope**. There are lots of beautiful works of art by famous artists here.

Homes

Most people in Italy live in towns or cities. The city of Naples grew up around a busy **port**. People left the countryside to come to Naples for work.

In the country, most houses have a small area of land around them. People can grow food for themselves or to sell.

Food

Many families enjoy eating together. For lunch they might eat cold meats with salad, **pasta**, bread, and cheese.

This pizzeria is in Rome.

Many delicious foods come from Italy.
Pizzas first came from Naples but now
most towns have a pizzeria. You can
watch the pizzas being made there.

Clothes

Many famous fashion designers come from Italy. Young people usually wear casual or sports clothes.

In the countryside people wear simple clothes. Some of the older Italian people always wear black.

Work

This farm in Sicily is growing oranges.

Some people work in farming. They grow wheat, fruit, and vegetables. Many workplaces close in the middle of the day because it is so hot.

In central and southern Italy many people work in shops and offices. Most of Italy's **factories**, where they make **products** such as cars or engines, are in the north.

Transport

Italy has good roads and **toll** motorways. It also has a very good train service. There are **ports** and airports too. Many young people ride **scooters**.

The city of Venice has **canals** instead of streets. People use boats called gondolas to get around.

Languages

Italy's **official language** is Italian. But different **regions** have their own **dialect**. The words in Italian are based on an old language called Latin.

The other main language is Sardinian.
This is spoken by people on the island
of Sardinia. Sardinian people also have
special clothes for festivals.

School

Primary school is for 6 to 11 year olds. School starts at 8.30 in the morning and finishes at about 1.00 in the afternoon. Pupils go to school six days a week.

Middle school is for 11 to 14 year olds.

The schoolday in middle school is longer and pupils usually have sports after school hours. Some pupils go to high school.

Free time

Most Italians love football. People of all ages talk about it and play it. There are big matches on Sunday afternoons.

In the early evening it is usual for people to meet up and walk around the main square or street in their town.

Walking around the square is called *passeggiata* (pa-se-jarta).

Celebrations

Every town in Italy has at least one festival. People take the day off work or school to watch a **procession** through the town.

The horse race in Siena is called the Palio.

On 2 July and 16 August there is a bareback horse race in Siena. Before the race, people parade around the main square in costumes.

The Arts

Italy has many **opera** singers and many Italians enjoy opera. Some of the operas take place in the **stadiums** built by the **ancient Romans**.

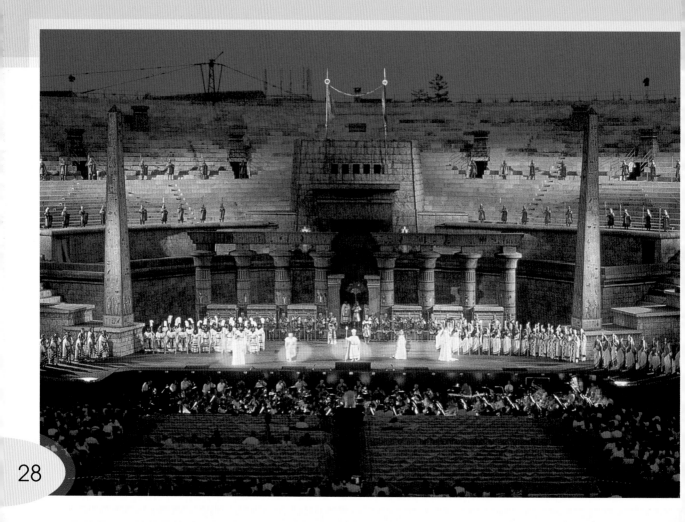

There are shows of puppets on strings as well as hand puppets.

The Punch and Judy show comes from the puppet shows that started in Italy hundreds of years ago. Today, puppet shows are still very popular in Sicily.

Factfile

Name   The full name for Italy is the Italian Republic.

Capital   The **capital** of Italy is Rome.

Language   Italy has two **official languages**: Italian and Sardinian.

Population   About 59 million people live in italy.

Money   Italian money is called the euro.

Religions   Almost all Italians are brought up as Roman Catholic.

Products   Italy produces wheat, vegetables, olives, wine, machinery, and clothes.

Words you can learn

uno (oono)	one
due (doo-ay)	two
tre (tray)	three
si (see)	yes
non (noh)	no
buon giorno (bwon JORno)	hello
arrivederci (a-ree-va-DAIR-chee)	goodbye
per favore (per-faVOR-eh)	please
grazie (graht-zee)	thank you

Glossary

ancient Romans the people who ruled most of Europe from Rome, over 2000 years ago

canal river dug by people

capital city where the government is based

dialect language spoken by people in one area

Europe the continent north of the Mediterranean Sea

factory building where things are made in large amounts

official language language that is used by the government and that is used in education

opera a play with music and singing

pasta a kind of dough that is made from flour and is cooked in boiling water. Spaghetti is a type of pasta.

Pope the head of the Roman Catholic Church

port place where ships pick up and drop off the goods they are carrying

procession a group of people walking along behind each other and often wearing costumes

product a thing which is grown, taken from the earth, made by hand or made in a factory

region area or part of a country

scooter small-wheeled motorbike

stadium large sports ground surrounded by seats

toll payment you have to make in some places for driving on the motorway

Index